# THE HIDDEN STORY OF
# HOMELESSNESS

## Karen Latchana Kenney

rosen publishing's

rosen
central®

New York

Published in 2014 by The Rosen Publishing Group, Inc.
29 East 21st Street
New York, NY 10010

First Edition

Produced for Rosen by Calcium Creative Ltd.
Editor for Calcium Creative Ltd.: Sarah Eason and Ronne Randall
Designer: Keith Williams

Photo credits: Cover: iStockphoto: Blue Cutler. Inside: Dreamstime: Alexraths 37, Amaviael 29, Americanspirit 33, 43, Annworthy 34, Anthonyata 27, Designpicssub 38, Gemenacom 20, Hurricanehank 31, Landd09 30, Leaf 23, Lisafx 40, Maxym022 36, Outline205 24, Pinkcandy 22, Wardrip Design 44, Wrangler 39; Shutterstock: Alexander Image 17, Robert J. Daveant 13, DJTaylor 18, Brian Eichhorn 9, Ejwhite 16, Glovatskiy 8, I4Icocl2 6, Lori Martin 10, Monkey Business Images 7, 15, Ildi Papp 14, Julia Pivovarova 28, Richard Thornton 4, Wrangler 1, 5, 12.

**Library of Congress Cataloging-in-Publication Data**

Kenney, Karen Latchana.
The hidden story of homelessness/Karen Latchana Kenney.—First edition.
    pages cm.—(Undercover story)
Includes bibliographical references and index.
Audience: Grades 5-8.
ISBN 978-1-4777-2797-3 (library binding)
1. Homelessness—United States—Juvenile literature. 2. Homeless persons—United States—Juvenile literature. I. Title.
HV4505.K378 2014
362.5'920973—dc23

2013021953

*Manufactured in the United States of America*

CPSIA Compliance Information:  #W14YA:  For further information, contact Rosen Publishing, New York, New York, at 1-800-237-9932.

# CONTENTS

# THE TRUTH ABOUT HOMELESSNESS

In cities and towns across the United States, people experience homelessness every day. Many see homeless people on the streets, but walk past the homeless as if they are invisible. It is a problem Americans have become used to seeing. However, it is a problem that is not going away and one that affects thousands of people each year.

Homelessness is simply not having a home. Someone might stay under a bridge or in a tent for shelter, but not every homeless person lives on the streets. A homeless person can find shelter in the homes of friends or relatives. However, that shelter is not permanent, and staying there is a temporary solution. It is still homelessness.

## ANYONE CAN BE HOMELESS

All ages and types of people can become homeless. It can happen to almost anyone. Homelessness has many causes. Sometimes the loss of a job causes a family to become homeless. One paycheck can mean the difference between having and not having a home.

*A man in Ventura, California, became homeless because of economic troubles in 2010.*

Sometimes domestic violence is the cause of homelessness. Women and their children may leave the family home to escape violence and become homeless as a result. Mental illness and substance abuse are other causes. There are even more reasons why people find themselves homeless.

People can experience chronic or temporary homelessness. Temporary homelessness is being homeless for less than a year. It is much more common than chronic homelessness, which is having a disabling condition, such as a severe mental illness, and being homeless for more than a year. It can also be having a disabling condition and having more than four episodes of homelessness in less than three years.

Being homeless makes it very hard for people to get their basic needs met. Hunger is a constant problem. Injury and illness are threats. Finding food, water, shelter, and warmth become the most important things to someone on the streets. Daily life is a struggle to survive. Homelessness affects society, families, teenagers, and young children. It is an issue that cannot be ignored.

*Life on the streets can be very difficult.*

# CHAPTER ONE

# NOWHERE TO GO

Karen lived in a quiet suburban neighborhood. It was not a place where homelessness was often seen. Her mom had mental health issues, however, and kicked Karen out one night. It was the first of many nights the 15-year-old found herself without a home.

*A woman gives money to a homeless girl in need.*

Karen slept on some friends' couches and even in someone's backyard. However, she was not allowed to stay in any one place for too long. She wandered the streets at night and tried to find heating grates. They were the best places to sleep. The warm air kept her from freezing during the long, cold night. It was a terrifying life for a teenager.

BREAKING NEWS

>> Just who is homeless? Here are the facts. From a one-day count across the United States in 2011, it was found that there were 636,017 people who were homeless.

*Many homeless people use signs to ask for money, food, work, or other help.*

## A COMMON STORY

Thousands of teenagers and children are made homeless every day in the United States. Many have parents with them, but many are alone on the streets. They might be homeless because they were kicked out of their homes by their parents, just like Karen. People may also become homeless for many other reasons.

The State of Homelessness in America 2012 report found that four groups of people had a high risk of becoming homeless. They were:
• People living with friends, family, or nonrelatives because they could not afford housing. • Released prisoners. • Young adults who have aged out of foster care. • People who do not have health insurance.

A stereotype about homeless people is that they are drug addicts or people who have mental health issues. This is true for many people experiencing chronic homelessness. It may also be the cause of their homelessness.

However, the chronic homeless make up around just 16 percent of all homeless people. Clearly, this stereotype is not a true representation of most homeless people in the United States.

### DIFFERENT REASONS

People become homeless for many reasons. Poverty or some kind of financial crisis are two major reasons. A job loss can cause missed rent or mortgage payments. Even if a person is working full time making minimum wage, he or she most likely cannot afford the rent required to house an entire family. If a medical emergency or the sudden death of a family member occurs, it can cause a family to become homeless overnight.

*Domestic violence is one cause of homelessness.*

**BREAKING NEWS**

>> **More homeless veterans end up living on the streets of Los Angeles than any other American city. The US Department of Housing and Urban**

Sometimes a person's family life is filled with abuse or conflict. Domestic violence can force women and children to leave their homes. Divorce, sexual abuse, or neglect can cause homelessness, too. Lesbian, gay, bisexual, or transgender (LGBT) teenagers who come out to their parents may not be accepted—many teenagers are thrown out of their homes because of their sexuality.

Veterans are another growing homeless group. Some soldiers come back from war with physical disabilities or mental health issues. As a result, it becomes difficult for them to maintain regular civilian lives. Sometimes these problems even lead to addiction or violence, and the veterans may lose their homes as a result.

*Some people become homeless due to mental illnesses or physical disabilities.*

Development reported in 2012 that 62,619 veterans were homeless on the night of the count. Of those, 6,371 were on the streets of Los Angeles.

Most people experience homelessness for only a short period of time. This is called transitional homelessness. Some sort of major crisis, such as a natural disaster, a job loss, or a medical condition usually causes transitional homelessness. This crisis causes a family or individual to become homeless. According to a 2012 US Conference of Mayors report, a lack of affordable housing was the leading cause of homelessness for families with children. Poverty, unemployment, eviction, and domestic violence were other leading causes.

*Many Hurricane Katrina flood victims lost their homes during the natural disaster.*

# UNDERCOVER STORY

## RICH EVANS'S STORY

Transitional housing isn't just a place to stay. Most transitional housing centers offer services that help people overcome their financial difficulties. For 22-year-old Rich Evans, his low-rent studio apartment at Nicollet Square in Minneapolis, Minnesota, gives him a chance to be independent after staying in emergency shelters and on couches for a year. The building offers job and life skills training and helps residents enroll in college. With the support of transitional housing, Evans hopes to pay off a student loan that was in default and return to college.

### A PLACE TO STAY

If families or individuals lose their homes, they most likely will spend some time with friends or family. They'll sleep on couches or in spare rooms. With this support, they can work and save money to get back into their own homes again. Without friends or family to offer a place to stay, some people have nowhere to go. These temporarily homeless people may sleep in their cars for a while or find a place that offers transitional housing.

Wherever they stay, people who are temporarily homeless usually find permanent housing within a year of becoming homeless. Homeless people such as these require temporary housing for only a short period of time. They are then able to support themselves once again.

People who are chronically homeless have very different needs. They need more than just a little time to get back on their feet. To stay in permanent housing, they may need help for the rest of their lives.

A chronically homeless person has been homeless for a long period of time. Most have a serious mental illness, a substance addiction, or a physical disability. They could be suffering from schizophrenia. This is a brain disorder that causes voices in a person's head and feelings of paranoia. It can be difficult for a person with this disorder to function in daily life. A chronically homeless person may have a severe addiction problem. A physical disability could also prevent someone from holding down a job and paying the bills. These are not problems that can be easily fixed.

*Chronically homeless people may never be able to live in permanent housing without support.*

BREAKING NEWS

>> Several Massachusetts communities have almost ended chronic homelessness in their areas. In 2007, Worcester released a plan to end chronic homelessness. The plan gave priority to housing

## THE HOMELESS CYCLE

The chronically homeless may spend decades going from hospitals to emergency shelters to living on the streets. They may even end up in jails. They cycle through different programs and treatments, ending back on the streets once more. These people require permanent housing help and other types of support to end their cycle of homelessness.

*A physical disability may prevent a homeless person from getting a job.*

chronically homeless individuals and adjusting housing restrictions to better fit them. Chronically homeless individuals also set their own goals to help end their homelessness. As of 2011, the plan was working, and most chronically homeless people in Worcester were living in permanent housing.

# CHAPTER TWO

# HOMELESS TEENAGERS

It can be hard to tell that someone is homeless. Lulu looks just like any other teenager—except she became homeless when she was 12. Before that she took care of her sick mother for four years. Lulu never met her alcoholic father, who never paid child support to her mother. Then Lulu's mom died from lung cancer in 2003. Lulu was the only one home when it happened. Her aunt and grandfather also died that year. Suddenly, Lulu was left alone to fend for herself.

*Being homeless is incredibly stressful for teens.*

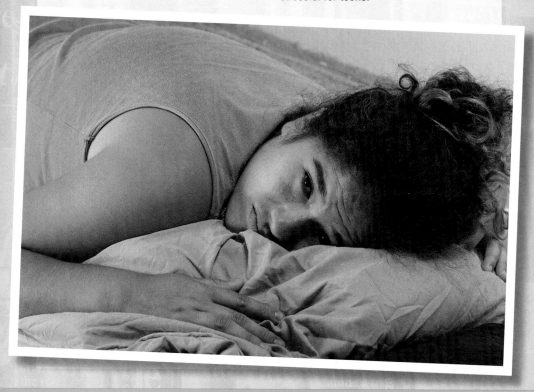

**BREAKING NEWS**

>> Establishing an accurate count of homeless teenagers is difficult. Most try to stay hidden. However, knowing their numbers helps the

Lulu went to 14 foster homes and seven group homes in the six years after her mom died. They were never places in which she wanted to stay. Lulu ran away from each home, ending up in Portland, Maine. There she met her boyfriend and moved in with his friend and family into a single, cramped apartment. She and her boyfriend paid the family $50 a week to stay there. It was either there or the shelter. However, Lulu was trying to find a place for her and her boyfriend. Soon there would be three of them—Lulu was pregnant.

## ONE OF MANY

Lulu is just one of many teenagers on the streets. The exact number of homeless youth at any one time is hard to estimate. This is because many teenagers don't use shelters—they are afraid they'll be sent into the foster care system. It's at shelters and other services where homeless counts are made.

*Homeless teens may not know where to go to find help.*

organizations that provide services to homeless people understand their needs. National homelessness counts range between 600,000 to 1.6 million each year.

Teenagers on the street are vulnerable. The street is a hostile environment for anyone, let alone a teenager. Most teenagers need help to survive. They become easy targets for adult predators, who can offer food, money, or a bed to sleep in. However, the results can be sexual, mental, and physical abuse. So, why do teenagers leave the safety of a home for the streets? They leave because many don't come from safe and supportive homes to begin with.

*Family problems are a major cause of teen homelessness.*

## BREAKING NEWS

>> Nearly 20,000 young people age out of foster care in the United States each year. Many have not completed high school or do not have a general education degree (GED).

## PROBLEMS AT HOME

Many homeless teenagers leave home because of problems within their families. There may be abuse in their home. This abuse might be domestic violence between parents. A parent or other family member may also sexually or physically abuse a teenager at home. Substance abuse by a parent or mental illness may be other causes of abuse.

*Many LGBT homeless youth report that family rejection is the cause of their homelessness.*

These disorders may result in the neglect of children in the home. A parent's job or home loss may also cause his or her teenager's homelessness.

Parents may reject their LGBT children when they come out. These teenagers may then be forced to leave their homes because of their sexuality. According to a 2012 report, nearly 40 percent of homeless young people are LGBT youth.

The foster, juvenile justice, and mental health systems often fail to support young people. These systems only support teenagers until they turn 18. Then they are released into the world to care for themselves. Many do not have any family or financial support system. These young people may also lack basic life skills.

Once they leave home, teenagers must quickly learn how to deal with life on the streets. Not having a home makes the most simple things much more difficult. Homeless teenagers must carry everything they need with them at all times. They have no place to store clothes, blankets, toothbrushes, or any other personal items they own.

Finding a dry, warm, and safe place to sleep is another immediate concern. Teenagers might sleep under bridges, in tents, or in abandoned garages or houses. These are not safe places to sleep, however. Some teenagers try to sleep during the day, when it's less likely they may be attacked. They stay awake at night and walk the streets.

*Many teens ask strangers for money to buy food.*

# UNDERCOVER STORY

## TEENAGE PANHANDLERS

Most homeless teenagers cannot work at a job. They may not be old enough or be eligible for different jobs, or keeping a job may become impossible. To get money for food, many homeless young people "panhandle." This means asking strangers to give them money. It can be humiliating for homeless people to panhandle, but it is a last resort in order to be able to buy food. Some people think panhandling should be made illegal. They believe it is a public nuisance.

## FINDING FOOD

Food and water are other constant concerns for homeless teenagers. If teenagers have money, they may be able to buy food. However, many do not and rely on strangers to give them food. These young people may also search for unused or leftover food that has been thrown in the garbage at restaurants.

Some desperate teenagers even steal food from stores.

Homeless young people do not have easy access to bathrooms or showers, so it becomes difficult for them to stay clean and wash their clothes. Being unclean is a problem in itself, because it can lead to a number of health issues.

School can be the one place homeless teenagers find stability, and many continue to go to school. According to the US Department of Education, there were more than 1 million homeless students enrolled in schools during the 2010–2011 school year.

However, school has its own difficulties for homeless students. Most don't want other students to know that they are homeless. They work hard to hide it from their friends. If found out, homeless teenagers are at risk of being bullied or teased. It is also very difficult for them to maintain their studies. They may not have a place to study, so they fall behind with their homework. They may not have a safe place to sleep, so they come to school exhausted. Sometimes they even fall asleep in class. Without access to transportation, it may also be difficult for these students to get to school every day. In addition to all this, the stress of being homeless affects their ability to do schoolwork.

*Homeless students may suffer emotionally and academically because of their situation.*

## SNOWBALL EFFECT

These substantial problems all add up, affecting how well homeless students do in school. Over time, being homeless can seriously affect a student's achievement. Students can develop learning problems and have low math and reading skills. If these problems are not addressed, these students leave school without the skills needed to succeed. They may fail to get jobs and become independent adults who can support themselves.

Teachers and school counselors can offer help to homeless teenagers, however. They can tell homeless students about available community services. Some schools offer special services for their homeless students. They include showering facilities, meals, clean clothes, and extended after-school activities.

# HITTING THE HEADLINES

## ONCE HOMELESS, NOW AT HARVARD

Some nights, newly homeless 15-year-old student David Boone slept on a wooden park bench in Cleveland, Ohio. Other nights, he "couch-surfed" at relatives' or friends' houses. However, he always did his homework and made it to school. His hard work paid off and he was accepted into 22 of the 23 colleges he applied to, including Princeton and Yale. His choice was Harvard. He started there in the fall of 2012, working toward an engineering degree.

# CHAPTER THREE

# SURVIVING HOMELESSNESS

When Tiffany's parents died, she went to live with her aunt and uncle. However, they didn't like the fact that Tiffany was a lesbian. She was kicked out of their home when she was just 15.

Tiffany was also being bullied in school because of her sexuality. She dropped out of school and fell into a deep depression. She tried to kill herself, overdosing on painkillers, Nyquil, and Tylenol PM. Tiffany survived the overdose, but surviving on the streets was hard. Some nights were spent sleeping on roofs during violent rainstorms.

*Teens can develop depression and other anxieties because of being homeless.*

Tiffany was on the streets for seven years. She's one of many young people who are kicked out of their homes for being gay.

BREAKING NEWS

>> Most homeless teenagers do not receive the health care that they need. Many also have multiple health problems. They have poor diets, which leads to malnutrition.

## STREET LIFE

Being on the streets is tough. Depression or other mental illnesses are common among homeless young people. They must watch their backs. They worry constantly, wondering where they can find food or sleep each night.

They miss having families and people who care for and love them. They also have to blend in with the homeless population to avoid sexual predators. There are many physical and mental dangers for homeless teenagers.

*Drug abuse is common among homeless teens.*

Some teenagers abuse substances, and many have emotional or mental issues. Some homeless young people develop chronic health issues because of their lack of medical care. These health issues include asthma, diabetes, and epilepsy.

The longer a teenager remains homeless, the more likely it is that homelessness will have serious health effects. It is physically demanding to be homeless. Without shelter, young people are exposed to harsh weather and temperatures. They may get frostbite or have wounds that do not heal fully. Being exposed can weaken people's immune systems. They are likely to get sick more often than housed teenagers, contracting bronchitis, pneumonia, or other illnesses. Homeless teenagers are also less likely to seek or receive medical care. They do not want to be returned to their families or be forced into foster care.

*Being homeless can cause serious long-term health issues.*

# HITTING THE HEADLINES

## FROM STAR TO HOMELESS ADDICT

Monet Monico was once a 19-year-old star on *The Suite Life of Zack and Cody* and *Zoey 101*. But after her father died, the star turned to heroin to deal with her pain. Her addiction led her to abandon acting and become homeless. She lived on the streets with her boyfriend, also an addict. Their days were spent using and trying to find more drugs to use. After being on the *Dr. Phil* show in August 2012, Monico went into treatment at Origins Recovery Center. As of February 2013, Monico had been clean and sober for more than 300 days. Addiction can cause homelessness, creating a cycle that is hard to escape.

### USING DRUGS TO COPE

Teenagers are also exposed to drug use while on the streets. They may have used before they were homeless or they may start while homeless. Some use drugs to cope with the stress and anxiety that comes with living on the streets. However, the drugs just end up making their problems worse. For some, the use turns to addiction. An addiction can make it even harder for teenagers to find permanent housing or a job. Dealing with an addiction usually also requires medical help. Coming off drugs is a difficult process for most people. It is even more difficult for a homeless person, who struggles to meet his or her basic needs every day. Addiction of any form also brings its own set of health issues.

Being homeless can make people feel invisible to society. Many people look past the homeless, as if they cannot see them. Homeless people can start to feel disconnected from society— as if they don't even belong to it anymore. It is important to remember that anyone can become homeless. This is a reality that most people don't want to face, so they choose to ignore it instead. However, feeling invisible and ignored can be emotionally difficult for homeless people and can wear down their self-esteem.

The feelings of alienation from society are why homeless teenagers try to connect with others on the street. It also helps to be part of a group. Then they are less vulnerable to dangerous adults. Homeless young people create street families—friendships with other, more experienced homeless teenagers. The more experienced teenagers teach the less experienced how to survive. They protect each other, but the protection usually comes at a price. These families may have abusive and unhealthy types of relationships, involving sex and substance abuse.

## UNDERCOVER STORY

## HOMELESS HATE CRIMES

A hate crime is an act of violence against a person or group of people based on someone's hatred for that type of person or group. Some people target the homeless for hate crimes. These crimes include beatings, rapes, and setting people on fire. The National Coalition for the Homeless found that hate crimes killed 32 homeless people in 2011. There were 105 hate attacks against homeless people in that year. Teenagers and young men committed nearly all of the attacks.

## USING SEX TO SURVIVE

Survival sex is one common problem with homeless young people. Many trade sex for food, clothes, money, or drugs. Most teenagers do not have money to buy what they need and do not want to go to shelters, so they believe sex is the most valuable thing they can trade. However, this sexual trade exploits vulnerable young people and can have terrible results. Teenagers may contract sexually transmitted diseases or find themselves with unwanted pregnancies.

*A homeless couple begs for help on a city sidewalk. Relationships between homeless teens can be based on survival, not love.*

Young people may leave home because they are being sexually or physically abused. They escape to the streets, but there they are at risk of even more abuse. According to the National Network for Youth, homeless young people are two to three times more likely to be raped or assaulted than other youth.

Predatory adults look for young people alone on the streets. These teenagers are vulnerable and scared. Predatory adults are adults who try to find young people they can lure to come with them to another place. They may promise homeless teenagers food, clothing, or money. They give them attention and may even tell them that they are special or loved. However, the predatory adults are not trying to help these teenagers. They want to sexually or physically abuse them. These predatory adults may be pimps, drug dealers, criminals, or ordinary-seeming people.

*The stress of being homeless can lead to mental illnesses.*

BREAKING NEWS

>> According to the National Center for Children in Poverty, approximately one in five homeless young people attempt suicide. More than half of

## MENTAL HEALTH ISSUES

Many homeless youth also have a mental illness. They develop emotional problems, such as depression and post-traumatic stress disorder (PTSD), as a result if their difficult experiences. They do not know how to deal with their physical or sexual abuse.

They have anxiety or high levels of stress, constantly worried about finding food or shelter. They also worry about being assaulted by strangers. Their mental illness may lead them to attempt suicide. Most do not receive medication or therapy to help with their illnesses.

*A homeless teen who is alone is vulnerable to predatory adults.*

heterosexual homeless teenagers have thoughts of suicide, and three-fourths of LGBT homeless youth have thoughts of suicide.

# CHAPTER FOUR

# GETTING OFF THE STREETS

Twelve-year-old Carissa ran from a bad situation at home to a bad one on the streets. Her stepfather was abusive, beating up her brothers and trying to abuse her sister. Her mother didn't do anything to protect Carissa and her 10 siblings. Carissa felt she had to leave.

Carissa bounced from group homes to juvenile hall to the streets. She was vulnerable and became a teenage prostitute. Her world was filled with violence, rape, and homelessness. Carissa was looking for loving attention, and sexual predators knew exactly how to exploit her.

*The help of an adult is important to teens who want to get off the street.*

**BREAKING NEWS**

>> Covenant House is a network of services and housing for homeless young people across North and Central America. It reports that up to 20,000 kids in the United States are forced into prostitution each year.

However, at juvenile hall, Carissa also gained the attention of mentors. These mentors would eventually save her from a life of violence and abuse. Counselors and teachers saw Carissa's great potential. They encouraged her to get an education and set goals for herself. Carissa did—and ended up achieving them all.

Carissa went to law school and then business school. She now speaks out about youth homelessness. She said, "And now with my story, with coming out and seeing the problem the way it is right now, I can do that for people that are voiceless, people that are homeless. Kids that are just invisible, I can stand up and fight for them and it's a wonderful feeling."

**HOPE FOR THE FUTURE**
There is always hope that a person can escape homelessness. Carissa escaped with the help of mentors. Homeless teenagers can find help in schools and shelters, youth programs, and religious organizations. Sometimes all it takes is just one person to make a huge difference in a homeless teenager's life.

*A homeless teen faces many obstacles to education and employment.*

Organizations provide different services to help homeless teenagers. Some places have van or street outreach programs in which members of the organization go to the streets to find homeless young people. They might give the teenagers a sandwich or tell them where they can get free, clean clothes. They'll also let homeless young people know what services their organizations provide.

Homeless shelters provide short-term services to homeless teenagers. The young people can get a bed for a night and free meals. They can take a shower and maybe get some new clothes. Teenagers can also talk with counselors. These counselors try to understand why these young people are homeless, offering advice or information to help them. The counselors can also help the teenagers reconnect with their families.

## CONTINUING HELP

Transitional housing helps homeless teenagers for longer periods of time. Homeless young people can continue with counseling and get help with their education. They can learn life skills and receive medical care. Teenagers can also get help with finding a job. The goal of transitional housing is to help homeless young people live independently. Different organizations focus on certain needs, such as teenagers who have addictions or single teenage mothers.

Permanent supportive housing is also available for homeless young people. It is generally for the chronically homeless who need support for their entire lives. They pay a small percentage of their rent. Government funding pays the rest of their rent.

*Opposite: Many homeless shelters provide holiday and other meals for people in need of food.*

>> According to the 2012 Point-in-Time Annual Homeless Assessment Report, on a single night in January 2012 there were:

- 229,206 beds available in emergency shelters.
- 197,192 beds available in transitional housing.
- 274,786 beds available in permanent supportive housing.

Some programs help teenagers develop specific skills, such as art or job skills. One café in Grand Junction, Colorado, helps homeless teenagers gain valuable job experience. The café is called Café V and it has partnered with a homeless shelter for teenagers. The vegetarian café hires teenagers from the shelter, giving them work opportunities that might be otherwise hard to find. Butter Bakery and Café, in Minneapolis, Minnesota, partners with local services to provide jobs and mentoring at-risk young people. These kinds of programs not only give homeless teenagers job training, but they also help boost their self-esteem.

*Art, such as legal graffiti, is a great way to connect with troubled teens.*

## CONNECTING THROUGH ART

Another great way to connect with homeless young people is through art. ArtStart is one program in New York City. It holds daily workshops for homeless young people. Local artists and teachers volunteer their time to develop art and music projects with homeless teenagers. The young people develop their artistic skills and also develop relationships with their mentors. Art can be an amazing tool through which to express a person's feelings. This is something that may be extremely difficult for homeless teenagers to do.

Different programs have a lot to offer to homeless teenagers. However, many teenagers avoid programs in an attempt to stay hidden, afraid they will be forced to go into foster care or back to abusive homes. By connecting with young people via their passions, such as art or music, programs can more easily reach vulnerable young people and deliver their services to them.

# UNDERCOVER STORY

## INOCENTE IZUCAR

The short documentary *Inocente* won an Oscar in 2013. It tells the story of Inocente Izucar, a homeless teenage artist in San Diego. She was in an art program called ARTS: A Reason to Survive. The program was a safe refuge for Inocente from her problems at school and with her mother. The documentary leads up to Inocente's first art show. The film changed her life, too. In 2012, Inocente was supporting herself by selling her paintings. Art was able to get Inocente off the streets and bring awareness to the problem of teenage homelessness.

# CHAPTER FIVE

# SOCIETY AND HOMELESSNESS

The problem of homelessness is growing, and some cities are responding with law enforcement. In these cases, laws that target the activities of homeless people are brought into force. These laws make it illegal to sleep, eat, sit, and panhandle in public spaces. Homeless people can then be arrested if found breaking these laws. Many cities employ extra officers to enforce the laws.

They hope that the laws will drive homeless people from their cities. According to the National Coalition for the Homeless, some of the toughest laws targeting homeless people are found in Sarasota, Florida, and Lawrence, Kansas. There it is illegal to sleep outdoors and panhandle.

*A homeless person can be arrested in certain states for lingering on the streets or asking for money.*

**BREAKING NEWS**

>> A 2008 study found that 60 percent of homeless young people in a New York shelter had been fined for offenses related to their homelessness.

## ENDING UP IN JAIL

The results of these laws are that homeless people end up in the criminal justice system. They spend time in jail and have criminal records. This can be especially damaging to young people who are placed in jails with tough criminals.

*Once arrested, teens may enter the justice system and gain criminal records.*

Some people believe arresting homeless people is not a solution to the problem at all. If anything, it just makes the problem worse. A criminal record makes it even harder for a homeless person to find employment or housing. The costs of the justice system are also higher than the costs of providing supportive housing. Is it right to arrest someone for not having a home? Many people believe it isn't. They believe it violates a homeless person's civil rights.

The offenses included panhandling and sleeping in a public space. The young people could not pay the fines, so warrants were issued for their arrest.

Communities recognize that homelessness is a growing problem. That's why there are many services available for the homeless. These services are offered at the local, state, and national levels.

Many churches and nonprofit organizations run programs to help the homeless. Individuals in communities donate to these charities. They might give clothing, money, or food. Then the charities distribute the goods to those in need. Some services help a person who is at risk of becoming homeless. They provide small grants to help with mortgage or rent payments. These local charities and organizations also run shelters, housing facilities, medical clinics, and food banks. The United Way is one large organization that provides funding for local and national programs that help the homeless.

*Different organizations feed, house, and counsel homeless teens and adults.*

## FEDERAL HELP

Federal funding comes from a variety of sources. The McKinney-Vento Homeless Assistance Grants program provides funding for homeless programs across the country. In 2012, more than $2 billion was budgeted for the program. It is the largest funding program for the homeless in the United States. The program emphasizes help for homeless families with children, homelessness prevention, and permanent supportive housing. The Homelessness Prevention and Rapid Re-Housing program also funds local and state programs. Its focus is on prevention and helping people move from shelters to independent living. There are several other federal programs that also fund different types of homeless services.

*Several federal programs provide funding to get people off the streets and into housing.*

# HITTING THE HEADLINES
# HOMES FOR HOMELESS VETERANS

Operation Stand Down Rhode Island is a community program that provides services for homeless veterans in the state. The program gives rental assistance and has housing facilities as part of its services. In 2012 the operation converted two properties into six homes for homeless veterans.

Prevention is one key factor to ending homelessness. Prevention for adults can mean receiving money to help with rent or mortgage payments during difficult times. A family can become homeless after missing just one of these payments. With small grants, families gain time to find work or figure out a plan to keep them from losing their homes.

*Counseling can help prevent a teen from becoming homeless.*

For teenagers, prevention may come in the form of intervention from a counselor or child welfare worker. If families are fighting, therapy may help solve their problems. Or in cases of neglect or abuse, a child welfare worker can place a teenager or child in a safer situation. Parents can also be educated about being more involved with their children's lives. If substance abuse or mental illness is affecting their children,

# UNDERCOVER STORY

## NATIONAL HOMELESS YOUTH AWARENESS MONTH

Every November, National Homeless Youth Awareness Month events are held in communities around the United States. Standup For Kids and YouthLink are two organizations that help spread the word about youth homelessness during the month. These and other organizations use social media, panel discussions, and blogs to spread awareness of the size of the problem.

they may be better able to notice the signs and offer help that will prevent their children from running away and becoming homeless.

### THE POWER OF MEDIA

The media are also a powerful tool for educating the public about homelessness. Documentaries look at the real lives of the homeless. The Spare Some Change media campaign focuses on the street youth in Los Angeles.

Through documentaries, public service announcements, street teams, and social media, the program spreads awareness of youth homelessness and connects homeless teenagers with mentors and people who can help them. This is just one of many media campaigns aimed at educating the public about homelessness. Just knowing about the problem can help prevent and solve the issue.

Homelessness can have some lasting effects on society. Without help, homeless teenagers can grow up to be troubled adults. Troubled adults may not reach their full potential and may not be able to contribute to their communities.

Since homelessness usually interrupts education, a homeless young person may educationally lag behind his or her peers.

This has a ripple effect that follows the teenager into adulthood. Without support, a homeless young person may not complete a high school education. College then becomes difficult or even impossible. Without education or job training, homeless teenagers can become unemployable adults, or people who may only be able to find jobs that do not pay a living wage. These adults then add to the US unemployment rate.

# HITTING THE HEADLINES
## VACANT HOMES FOR THE HOMELESS?

Due to hard economic times, many cities are filled with vacant homes. Some city authorities are considering housing the homeless in those vacant homes. Some believe this would be the ideal solution to the problem of homelessness, especially since there are so many vacant homes. According to Amnesty International, there are more than five times as many vacant homes as there are homeless people in the United States.

## THE CRIMINAL CYCLE

If homeless young people enter the justice system because of being homeless, it can be more damaging than helpful. Many kinds of criminals are in the justice system. Homeless young people are exposed to violence and different kinds of criminal activity in jail. Many homeless teenagers are treated like dangerous criminals. It also costs more to keep a homeless young person in jail than it costs to provide housing.

One Colorado study found that it costs around $5,887 to permanently keep a youth off the streets. The study found that it cost $53,665 to keep a youth in jail for a year. Once the person leaves the justice system, it may be even harder to move back toward an independent life in society. As an adult, the homeless person may simply find themself back in jail again.

*Some cities are considering fixing up vacant homes to house the homeless.*

# HOMELESSNESS—THE TRUTH

Being homeless is not something anyone wishes for, but it's a situation that many people face every year. Homelessness affects all kinds of people—from the man who loses his job to the teenager trying to escape abuse at home. People become homeless for many different reasons. Sometimes substance abuse is involved, or a parent cannot find a job that pays enough to rent a home for his or her family. Sometimes a parent cannot accept a teenager's sexuality, and forces the young person to leave his or her home. Whatever the reason, the reality of life on the streets is harsh.

*With help, homeless teens can make it off the streets to become independent and successful adults.*

# UNDERCOVER STORY

## PAULINA'S JOURNEY

Paulina bounced from one foster home to another. She was in her ninth foster home and her foster mother was using Paulina as a babysitter for her kids. Paulina finally refused and she was kicked out. That's when Paulina found Covenant House. The counselors and housing there helped her get back on her feet. She made her way into college and a job. Finally, she had hopes for her future. Her goals were to finish college and start a career.

### PROBLEMS ON THE STREET

Homeless teenagers face many dangers on the street. They are exposed to adult predators and drug use. They have to find ways to meet their basic needs of food, water, and shelter. They may resort to stealing, panhandling, or even survival sex to get by. They must also try to stay in school, do homework, and study while dealing with being homeless. The stress and fear can lead to mental illnesses. Homelessness can also lead to many health problems, including malnutrition and asthma.

There are services available to help homeless teenagers. Getting those services to the teenagers can be challenging, however. Many want to remain hidden from the system, to avoid being sent back home or into foster care. With help, homeless teenagers can find a path off the streets. With support, they can look forward to finding a bright and independent future.

# GLOSSARY

**addiction** A condition in which the body and mind crave and depend on particular substances, such as food, drugs, or alcohol.

**anxiety** Feelings of worry or fear.

**chronic** Something that does not get better for a long time.

**disability** A physical condition that limits the way a person moves or feels things.

**domestic violence** Violence that happens in the home or between family members.

**foster care** Care for a child by an adult or adults who are not the child's legal parents, in the adults' home.

**frostbite** Damage done to parts of the body, such as fingers or toes, that is caused by extremely cold temperatures.

**mortgage** A loan given by a bank to buy a home.

**nuisance** Something that annoys or causes problems for someone.

**panhandle** To beg for money on the street.

**poverty** Being poor.

**predator** A person who wants to exploit others.

**prevention** Stopping something from happening.

**prostitution** Having sex with someone in exchange for money.

**sexually transmitted disease** A disease that is spread through sexual contact.

**stereotype** An overly simplified picture or opinion of a person or group.

**survival sex** Trading sex for food, clothing, shelter, or other things a person needs to survive.

**therapy** Treatment for a disability, illness, or injury.

**transitional** A place or time where or when something or someone changes from one form to another.

**vulnerable** Being in a weak position.

# FOR MORE INFORMATION

## BOOKS

Barber, Nicola. *Fighting Poverty*. Chicago, IL: Heinemann Library, 2013.

Bringle, Jennifer. *Homelessness in America Today*. New York, NY: Rosen, 2011.

Gay, Kathlyn. *Volunteering: The Ultimate Teen Guide*. Lanham, MD: Scarecrow Press, 2004.

Green, Robert. *Poverty*. North Mankato, MN: Cherry Lake, 2008.

Stearman, Kaye. *Taking Action Against Homelessness*. New York, NY: Rosen Central, 2010.

## ORGANIZATIONS

**Teen Line**
P.O. Box 48750
Los Angeles, CA 90048
(310) 855-HOPE (4673) or (800) TLC-TEEN (852-8336)
Web site: http://teenlineonline.org
A site and phone line run for teens by teens that deals with a variety of issues that affect young people.

**U.S. Department of Housing and Urban Development**
451 7th Street S.W.
Washington, D.C. 20410
(202) 708-1112
Web site: http://portal.hud.gov:80/hudportal/HUD?src=/program_offices/comm_planning/homeless
The U.S. Government has a program dedicated to helping homeless people find housing, food, training, and counseling to end the cycle of homelessness.

## WEB SITES

Due to the changing nature of Internet links, Rosen Publishing has developed an online list of Web sites related to the subject of this book. This site is updated regularly. Please use this link to access the list:

http://www.rosenlinks.com/UCS/Home

# INDEX